BRAIN GAM

Easy

MAZES

pil
Publications International, Ltd.

Cover puzzles: Tim Bohmann, Myles Callum, Adrian Fisher

Puzzle creators: Alexandr III, Cihan Altay, Tim Bohmann, Michael D. Brown, Myles Callum, Julie Cohen, Don Cook, Adrian Fisher, Connie Formby, Peter Grosshauser, Bob Harris, David Helton, Robin Humer, Steve Karp, The Maze Generator Website, Patrick Merrell, Carla Nichiata, Adrian Niederhaeuser, Poosan, Ratselmeister, Marilyn & DC Roberts, Pete Sarjeant, Andrew Scordellis, Jen Torche, VanDenBlind, Iva Villi, Alex Willmore, Igor Zakowski

Puzzle illustrators: Helem An, Chris Gattorna, Elizabeth Gerber, Jessi LeDonne, Jen Torche

Brain Games is a registered trademark of Publications International, Ltd.

Louis Weber, CEO
Publications International, Ltd.
7373 North Cicero Avenue
Lincolnwood, Illinois 60712

Permission is never granted for commercial purposes.

ISBN: 978-1-4508-8401-3

Manufactured in U.S.A.

8 7 6 5 4 3 2 1

A-maze-ing Fun!

You don't have to look much further than a local cornfield each fall to find evidence of the popularity of mazes. Mazes have fascinated and delighted people for centuries. People have cultivated them out of hedges, built them with brick and mortar, crafted them in amusement parks using paths lined with mirrors, and yes, even plowed perplexing pathways in fields of—you guessed it—maize.

The twists and turns your mind takes while working these mazes aren't just for fun. These mazes are actually good for you, as well! Exercising your brain by solving mazes and other puzzles can help increase your mental flexibility and build focused attention and problem-solving skills.

Brain Games®: Easy Mazes is packed with more than 160 mazes. The focus in this book is fun, so we've left out the overly difficult mazes. Instead, you'll find a variety of easy, approachable mazes that will give your mind the exercise it needs without leaving you frustrated and defeated.

The most important thing to do with this book is to enjoy yourself. Don't worry too much if you hit a dead end. Answers are conveniently located in order in the back of the book. Some mazes have alternate solution paths, so your route may differ from the answer provided.

If you'd like to give your eyes a rest while still enjoying the mental workout a good maze can provide, it's time to sit back and relax with *Brain Games®: Easy Mazes*.

MAZE 1

Only one of the 3 pieces (labeled A, B, and C) will allow you to go from start to finish without getting stuck. Which one is it?

START

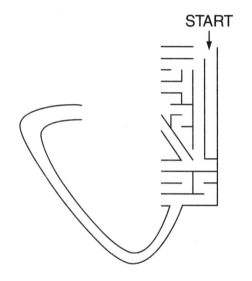

A

B

C

END   END   END

MAZE 2

Find your way through the maze with the fewest number of bounces. Keep going forward until your way is blocked; at that point, you can only turn left or right.

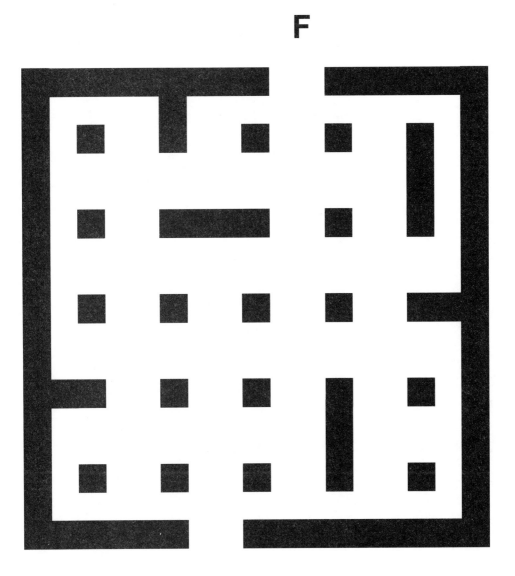

MAZE 3

Can you make your way through this maze?

You're on a runaway train that won't stop moving forward! The path from start to finish must follow the curve of the loops; sharp turns aren't allowed.

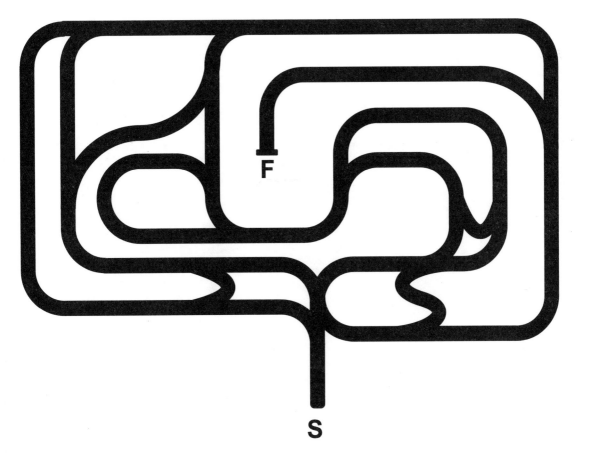

MAZE 5

Find your way through these crazy circles!

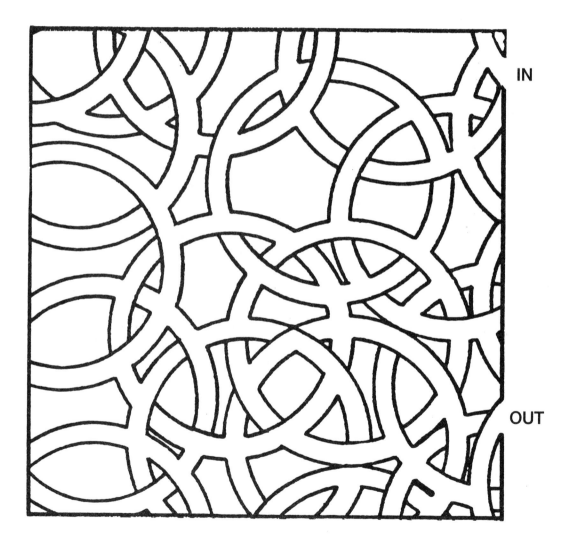

IN

OUT

MAZE 6

The taxi meter is ticking. This professional building is a maze of corridors and cubicles. Elevators are local or express only; there are no stairs. And over-stressed office workers won't give you directions to the exit. Why, oh why, did you ever come in here? Doesn't matter now—time to get moving!

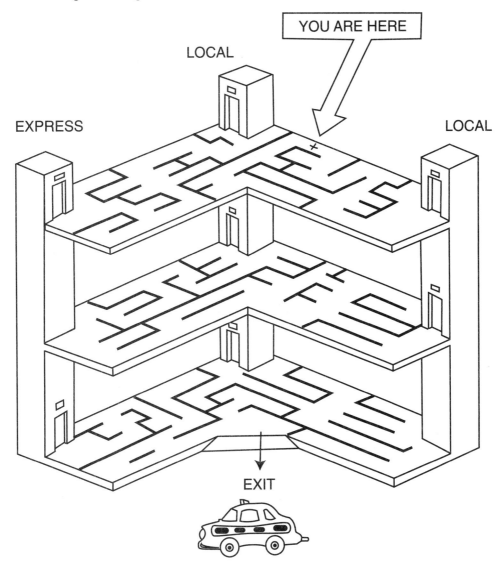

MAZE 7

Moving diagonally, can you find a single, unbroken path from the circle in the upper left corner to the diamond in the lower right? Your path must alternate between circles and diamonds. There's only one way to do it.

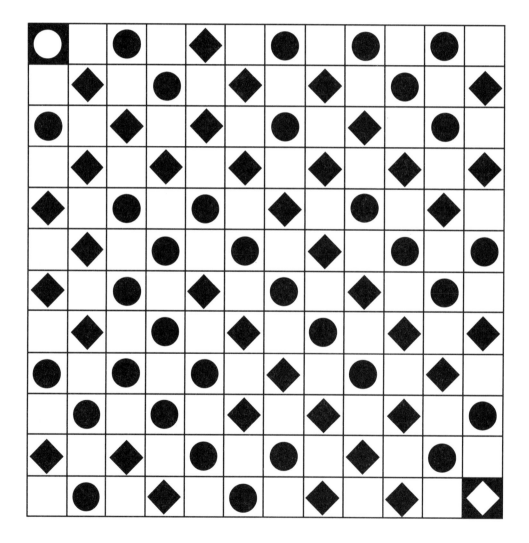

MAZE 8

Can you find your way to the center of this maze?

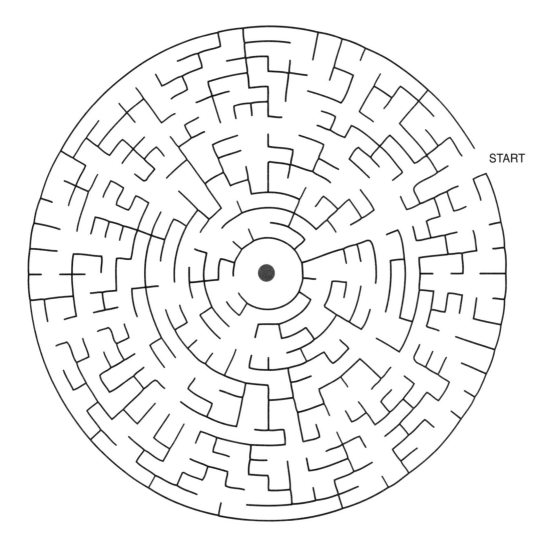

START

MAZE 9

Follow the slugger's blast to the ball's location in the center and then out of the park!

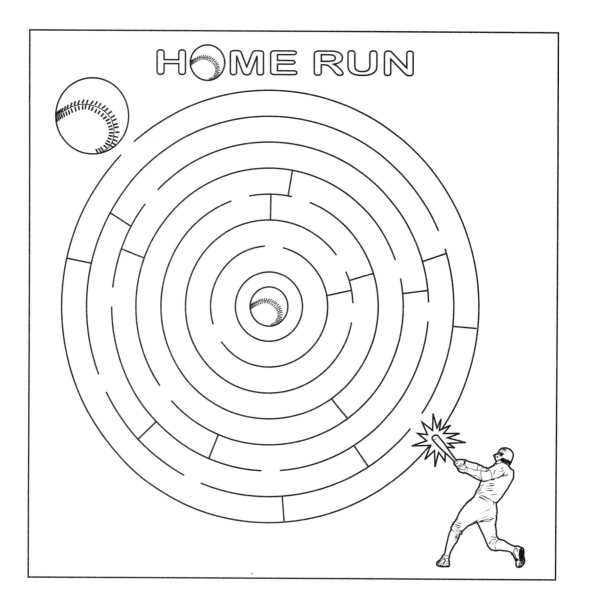

MAZE 10

Don't get too caught up in all the twists and turns as you negotiate your way to the center of this intricate labyrinth.

MAZE 11

Starting at the top left, navigate your way to the bottom of this maze. Prepare for plenty of zigs and zags!

MAZE 12

Can you find your way through this sea of cubes?

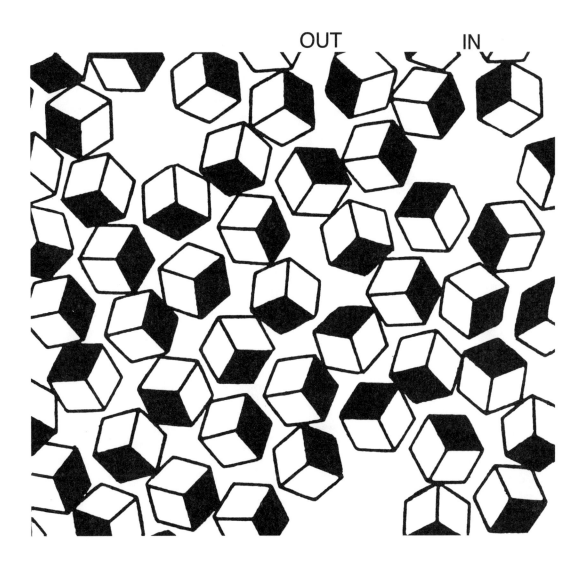

OUT   IN

MAZE 13

Negotiate your way through this intricate airplane labyrinth.

MAZE 14

Doesn't this maze look like a screen seen in Chinese restaurants? All you have to do in this maze is enter at the top left and come out the bottom right as quickly as possible.

MAZE 15

Help the little fish swim through the brain coral so he can get away from the bigger fish.

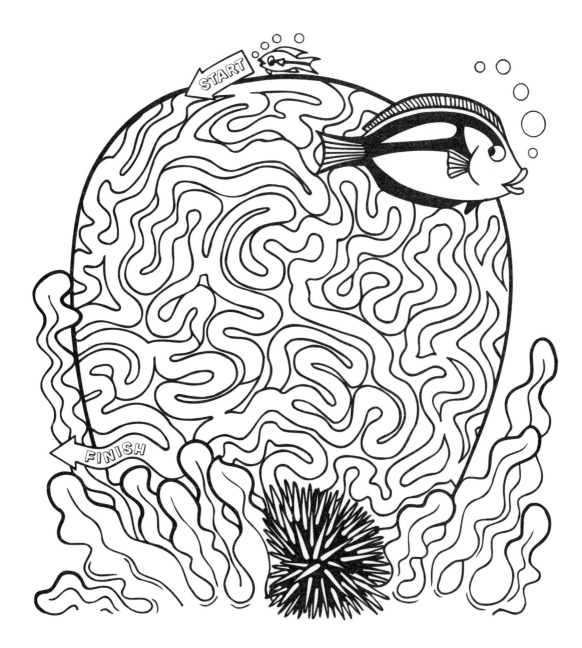

Don't let its function confuse you as you make your way through this computer chip.

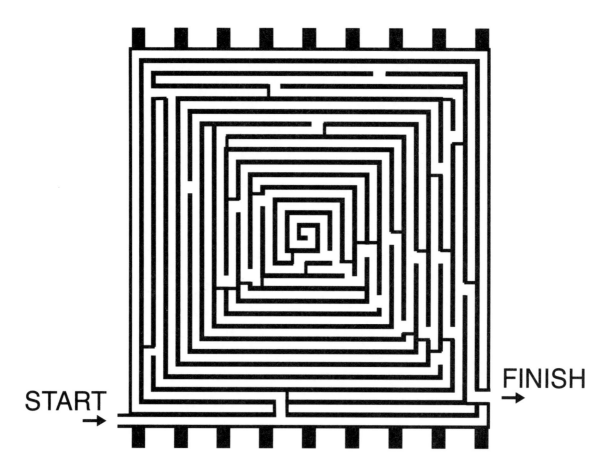

START →

FINISH →

MAZE 17

Climb up, dig down, and make your way through this pyramid to the treasure below.

MAZE 18

Find your way through the maze with the fewest number of bounces. Keep going forward until your way is blocked; at that point, you can only turn left or right.

MAZE 19

Follow the slugger's blast to the ball's location near the top of the maze.

MAZE 20

Only one of the 3 pieces (labeled A, B, and C) will allow you to go from start to finish without getting stuck. Which one is it?

START

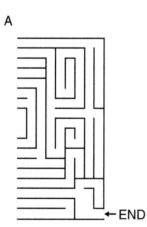

A

B

← END

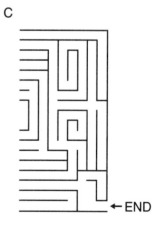

C

← END

← END

MAZE 21

Line up the putt to get a hole in one as you go through the maze.

MAZE 22

Navigate the twisting path to find your way through this maze.

end

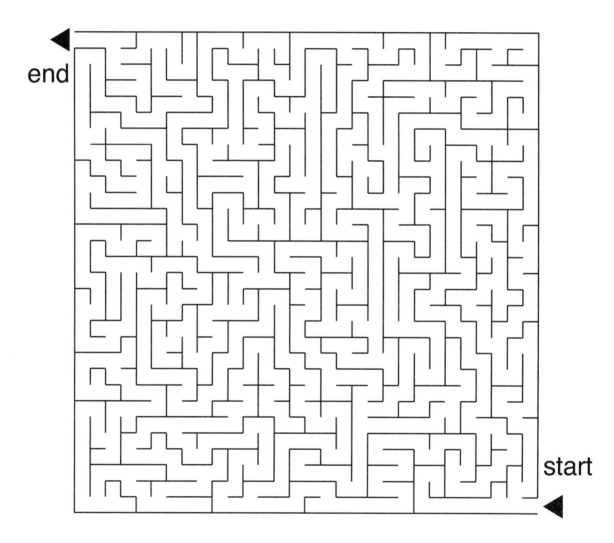

start

MAZE 23

Connect the dots by finding your way through this circular maze.

25

MAZE 24

Your tractor is jammed and you can only go forward or turn left!

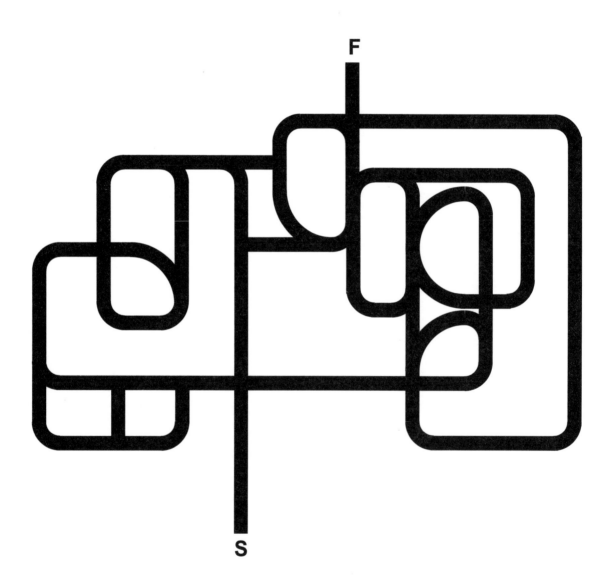

MAZE 25

Do your best to buzz right through this honeycomb maze. Please "bee" careful!

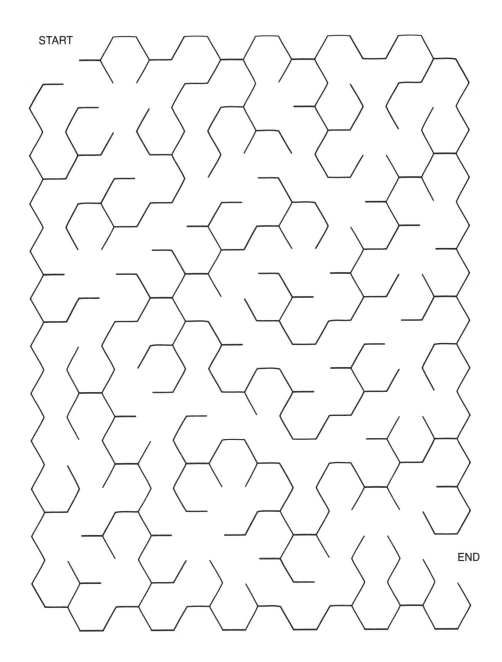

START

END

MAZE 26

See how quickly you can get this mouse through the maze to the cheese on the other side.

MAZE 27

Don't get too caught up in all the flashing lights as you find your way out of this slot machine.

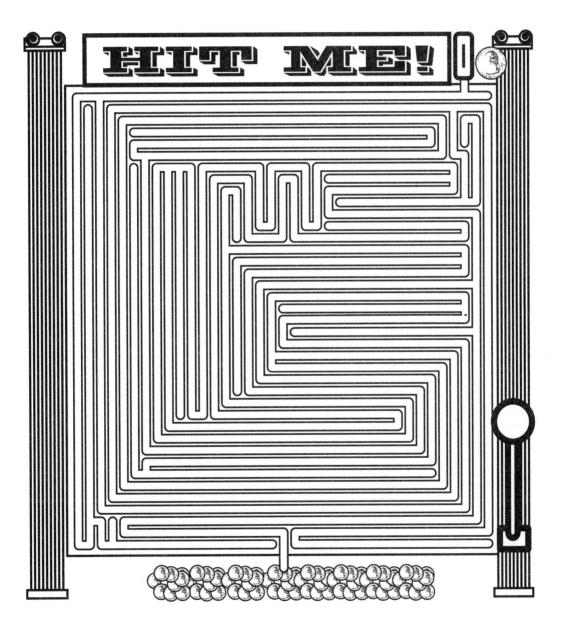

Draw a single closed path passing through each empty cell of the grid exactly once and moving only horizontally and vertically.

MAZE 29

Guide the path of the ball to the fielder's mitt.

MAZE 30

This professional building is a maze of corridors and cubicles. Elevators are available, but there are no stairs. And over-stressed office workers won't give you directions to the exit. Why, oh why, did you ever come in here? Doesn't matter now, because it's time to get moving—the taxi meter is ticking!

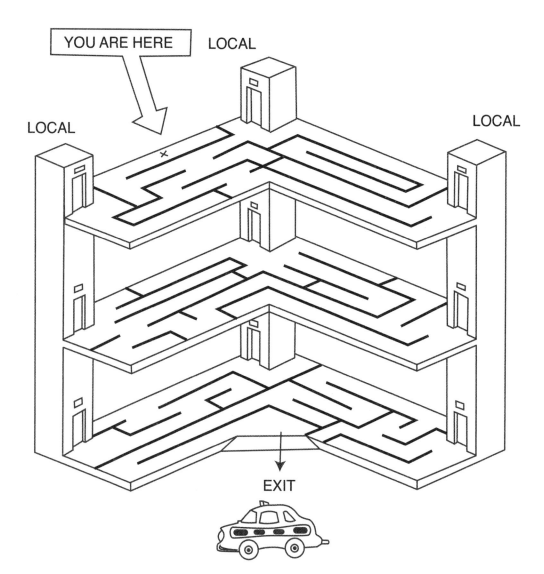

MAZE 31

Some prankster has taken an octagonal stop sign and painted a maze over it. The Traffic Fairy says it can be restored only if you can find the shortest way into the center. Hint: There is a bridge you can go under and over (where there is a line instead of a wall).

MAZE 32

You've caught something! Guide your line to the surface and retrieve the fish.

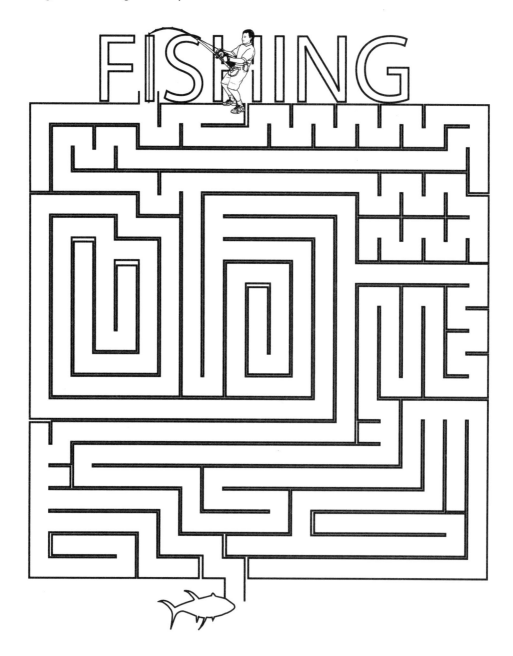

MAZE 33

Find your way through the maze with the fewest number of bounces. Keep going forward until your way is blocked; at that point, you can only turn left or right.

F

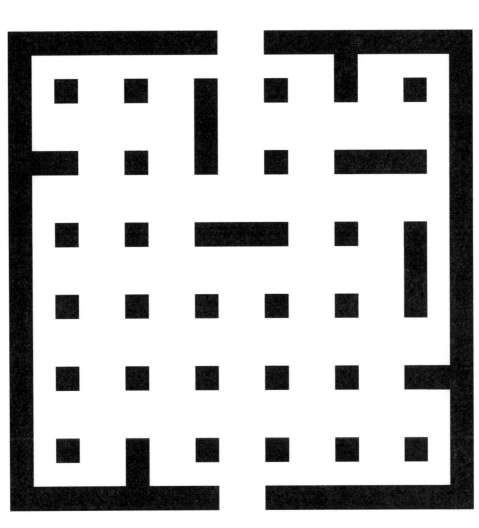

S

This ship's going down! Guide the final crewman to the exit at the bottom (now the top) of the ship for an aerial rescue.

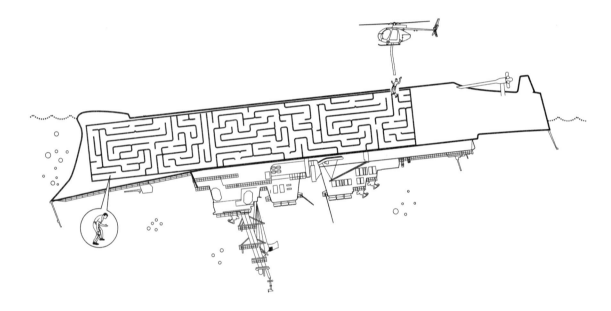

MAZE 35

Start your way at the top left of this maze and exit on the bottom right. There are so many twists and turns you might think you're in aerobics class.

START

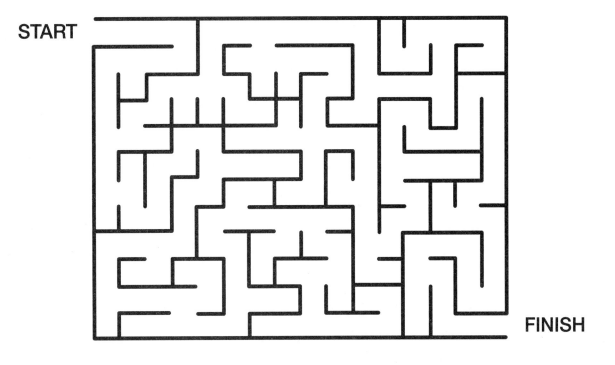

FINISH

37

MAZE 36

Lead the bee through each flower to gather pollen, then get to the beehive in a hurry.

START

FINISH

MAZE 37

Navigate your way through the maze to safely land the helicopter on the "X."

MAZE 38

Guide the path of the ball to the slugger's bat.

MAZE 39

Dig your way through the center of the earth from Australia to Spain.

MAZE 40

Navigate the twisting path to find your way through this maze.

start

end

MAZE 41

Help the river otter get dinner by finding a clear path to the crayfish.

MAZE 42

Run your train through the maze entering and exiting with the arrows. You can't back up, and you can't jump the track at the crossovers—you must go straight through them.

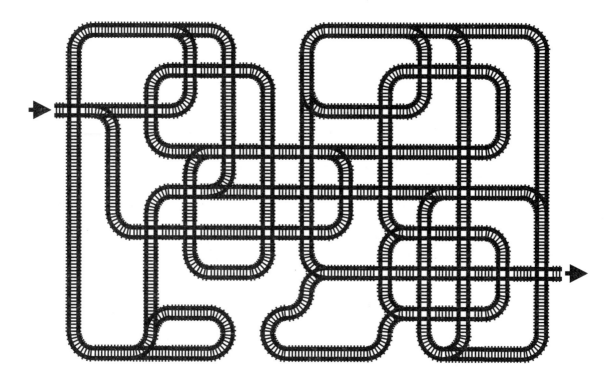

MAZE 43

Can you make your way from the start to the black-hole finish?

FINISH

START

MAZE 44

There's nowhere to go but up in this maze, although you will make plenty of left and right turns in the process.

MAZE 45

You're on a runaway train that won't stop moving forward! The path from start to finish must follow the curve of the loops; sharp turns aren't allowed.

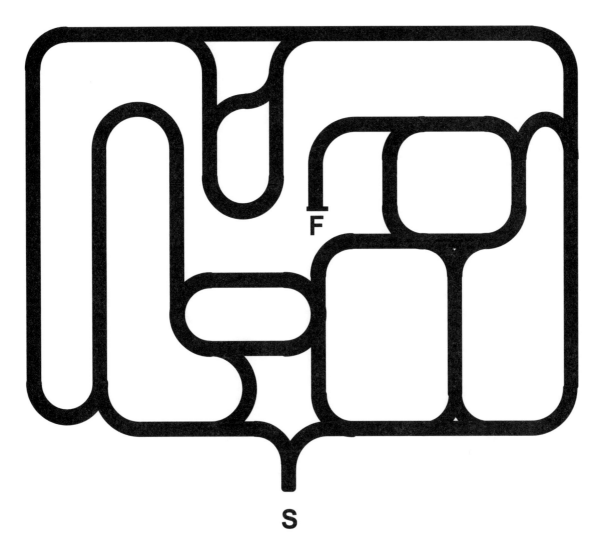

MAZE 46

To solve this maze, just imagine you're on one of those survival-type shows. Your team and your rival team have been led, blindfolded, to the center. Now the blindfolds are off, and you have to find your way out. The team that negotiates this puzzle fastest wins. How soon can you get out?

MAZE 47

Don't get too caught up in all the twists and turns as you negotiate your way through this patriotic labyrinth.

MAZE 48

Don't run out of time! Help the mouse find the cheese at the end of the maze.

MAZE 49

Only one of the 3 pieces (labeled A, B, and C) will allow you to go from start to finish without getting stuck. Which one is it?

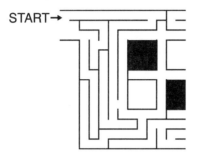

START→

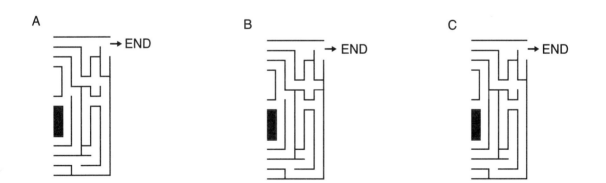

A

→ END

B

→ END

C

→ END

MAZE 50

Can you loop your way in and out of this maze?

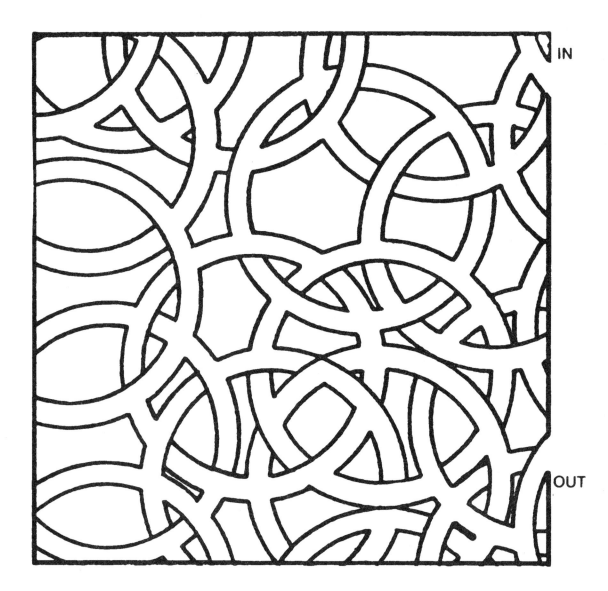

IN

OUT

MAZE 51

Please help George find his way to room 34 for his computer class.

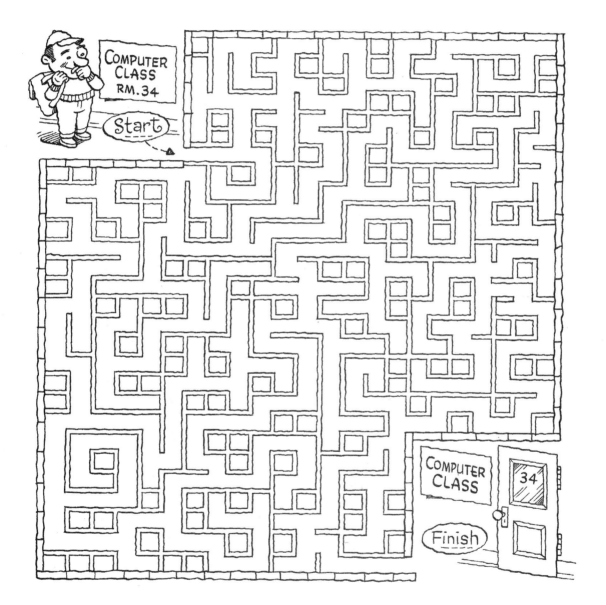

MAZE 52

You need to get to the center of the pentagon to give top secret information to the chief and then dash out the back way. Can you find your way?

MAZE 53

Find the path to the fielder's mitt.

MAZE 54

Navigate the twisting path to find your way through this maze.

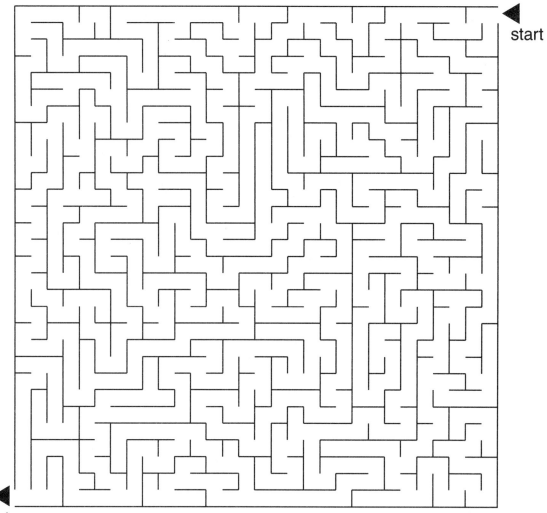

start

end

MAZE 55

Find a path from the black dot in the top colored square to the gray square at the bottom-right corner.

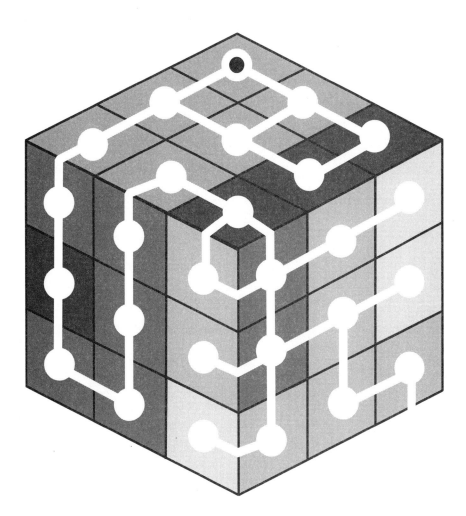

MAZE 56

You've caught something! Guide your line to the surface and retrieve the fish.

It's trouble in the sea! Help the little fish escape the octopus.

MAZE 58

Can you get from Alaska to Zanzibar? Actually, we'll settle for A to Z.

MAZE 59

Help this quarter find its way through the inner workings of this slot machine. You just may hit the jackpot along the way!

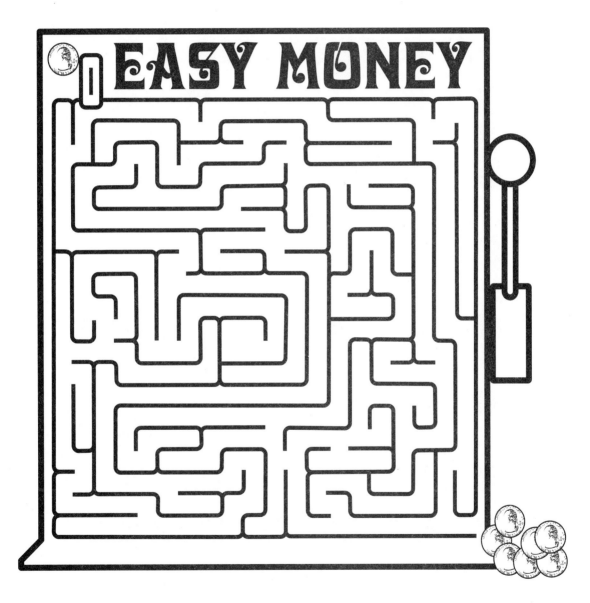

MAZE 60

Find your way through the maze with the fewest number of bounces. Keep going forward until your way is blocked; at that point, you can only turn left or right.

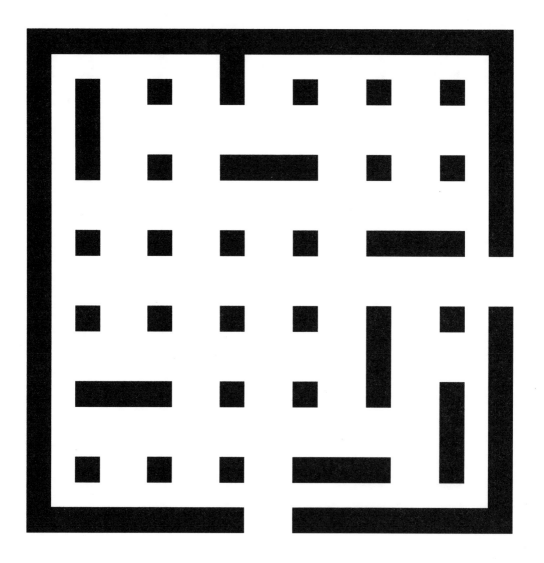

F

S

62

MAZE 61

Line up the putt to get a hole in one as you go through the maze.

Find your way through the tangled maze.

MAZE 63

Spin your way through this record maze.

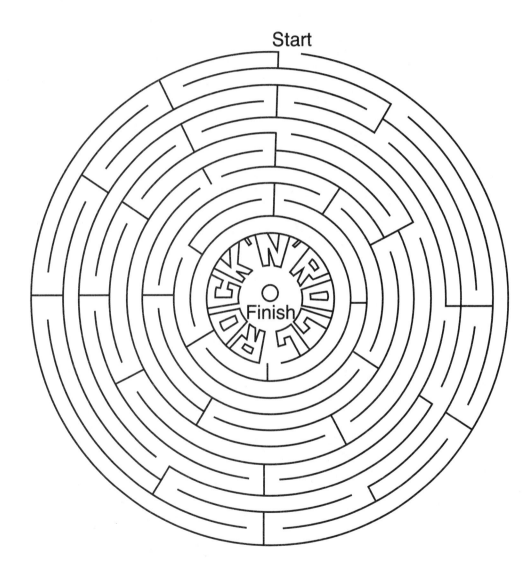

MAZE 64

This maze might look tough, but it's really a cakewalk.

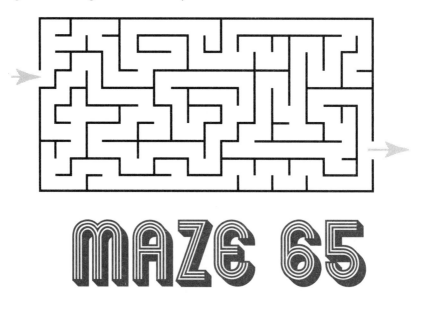

MAZE 65

The taxi meter is ticking. This professional building is a maze of corridors and cubicles. Elevators are available, but there are no stairs. And over-stressed office workers won't give you directions to the exit. Why, oh why, did you ever come in here? Doesn't matter now—time to get moving!

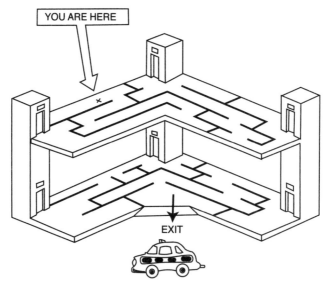

YOU ARE HERE

EXIT

MAZE 66

This mom is trying to order pizza for her kids. Can you guide her call? Be careful not to get the wrong number!

MAZE 67

Travel back in time through a dinosaur's body!

MAZE 68

This ship's going down! Guide the final crewmember to the exit at the bottom (now the top) of the ship for an aerial rescue.

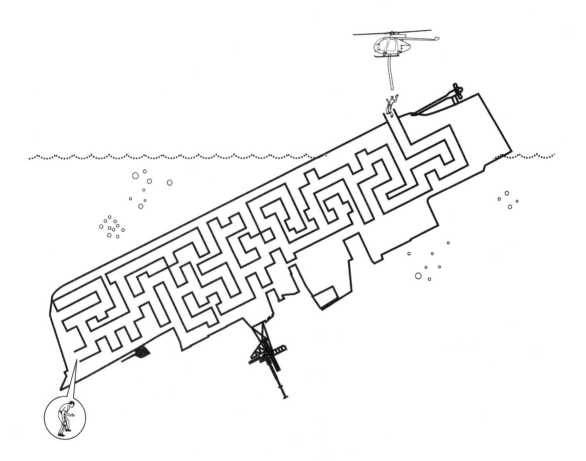

MAZE 69

Get from A to B as quickly as possible.

A

B

MAZE 70

Negotiate your way through this intricate labyrinth.

MAZE 71

Follow the slugger's blast to the ball's location at the top left of the maze.

MAZE 72

Your tractor is jammed and you can only go forward or take a soft left! Can you find your way through the fields?

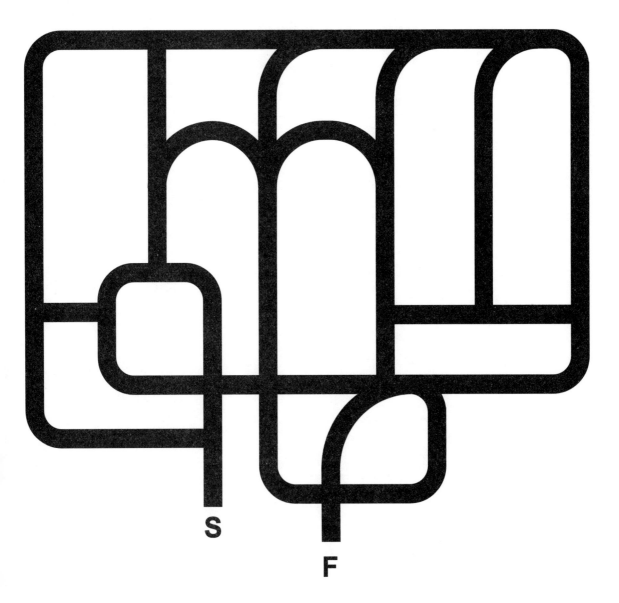

S

F

MAZE 73

Nothing eases the Monday-morning blues like a donut. If you can find your way through this maze, you'll be on your way to a great week!

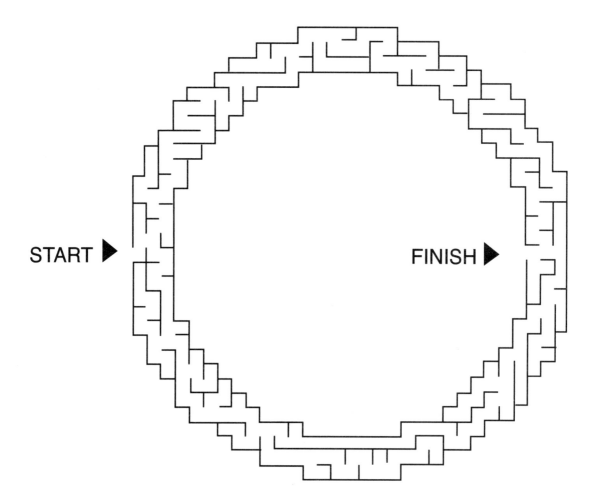

START ▶

FINISH ▶

MAZE 74

You can solve this crossword in record time, because we've removed the clues and turned it into a maze, instead. Start at the top left.

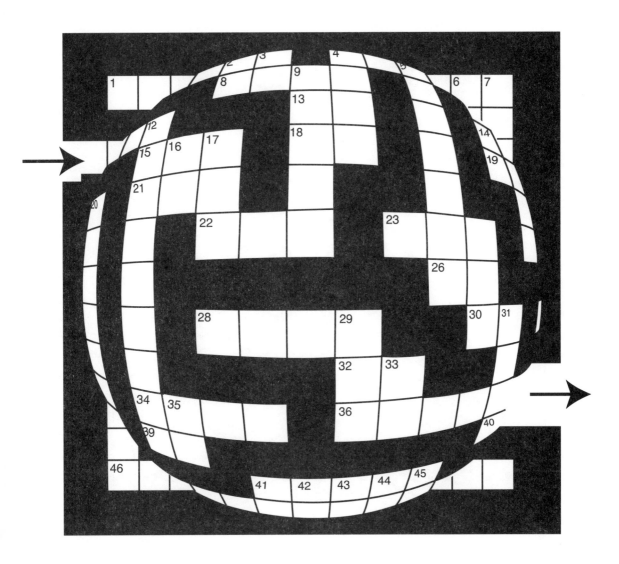

MAZE 75

The taxi meter is ticking. This professional building is a maze of corridors and cubicles. Elevators are local or express only; there are no stairs. And over-stressed office workers won't give you directions to the exit. Why, oh why, did you ever come in here? Doesn't matter now—time to get moving!

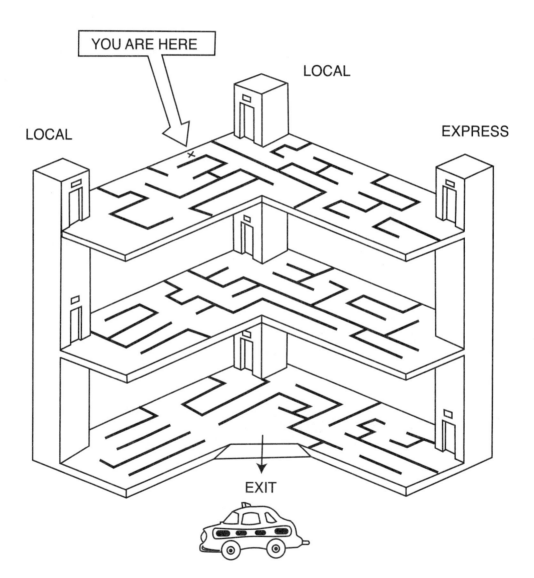

MAZE 76

Navigate the twisting path to find your way through this maze.

start

end

MAZE 77

Find your way through the maze with the fewest number of bounces. Keep going forward until your way is blocked; at that point, you can only turn left or right.

F

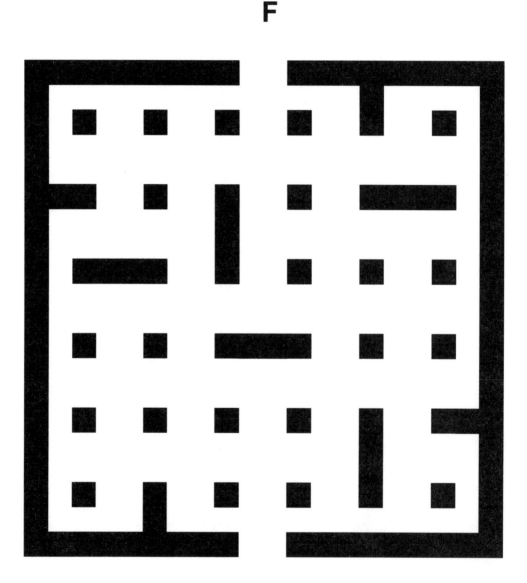

S

78

MAZE 78

Help this explorer locate the center of the moon where he hopes to find precious metals.

All you have to do to solve this puzzle is move in a single, unbroken path from the circle in the upper left corner to the circle in the lower right. Your path must alternate between circles and squares, and you can only move horizontally and vertically (not diagonally). There's only one way to do it.

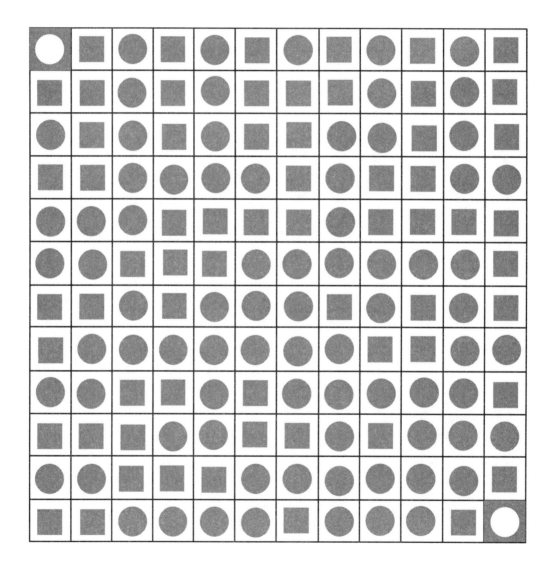

MAZE 80

Cross over and under bridges to reach the end of this maze.

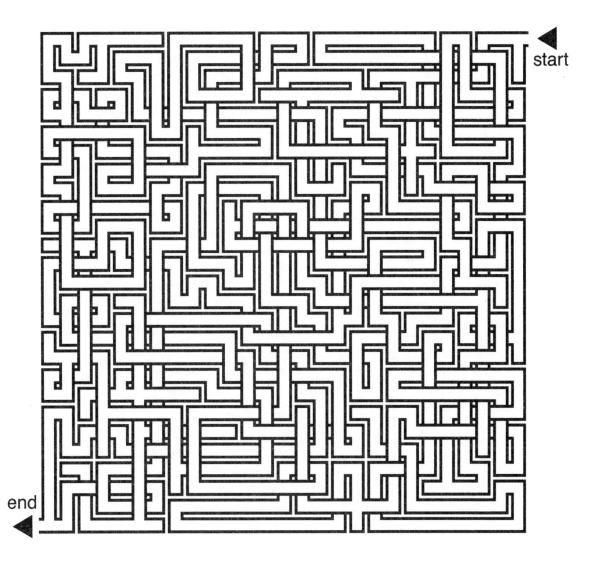

start

end

MAZE 81

Guide your way through the loops and tangles of this circuitry maze.

START

FINISH

This confused driver is having trouble finding the gas station—and he's running on empty!
Follow the arrows to help him find the correct route.

MAZE 83

Find the path to the fielder's mitt.

MAZE 84

The man with the snacks in the upper-right corner needs a little assistance avoiding obstacles so he can get back to his seat in the bleachers and enjoy the game. Can you help him?

MAZE 85

Connect the dots by traveling through the circle maze.

MAZE 86

Find your way through this haunted maze—if you dare!

OUT

IN

Connect the dots in this Tudor rose. Hint: Follow the lines, not the space between them.

MAZE 88

Navigate the twisting path to find your way through this maze.

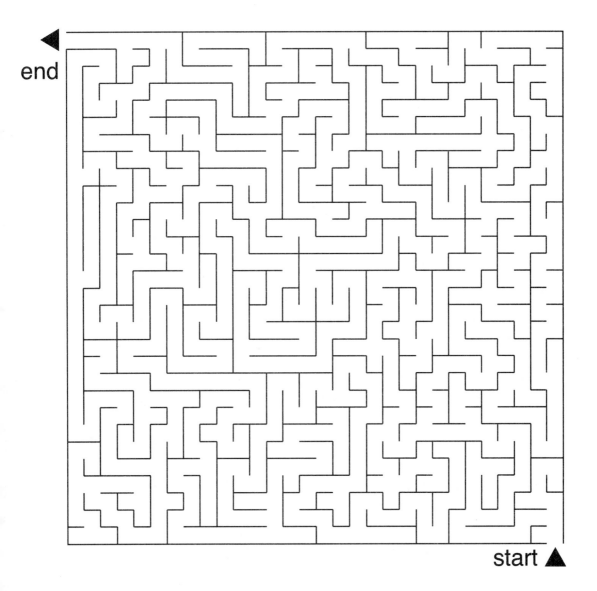

end

start

MAZE 89

Find your way through the maze with the fewest number of bounces. Keep going forward until your way is blocked; at that point, you can only turn left or right.

F

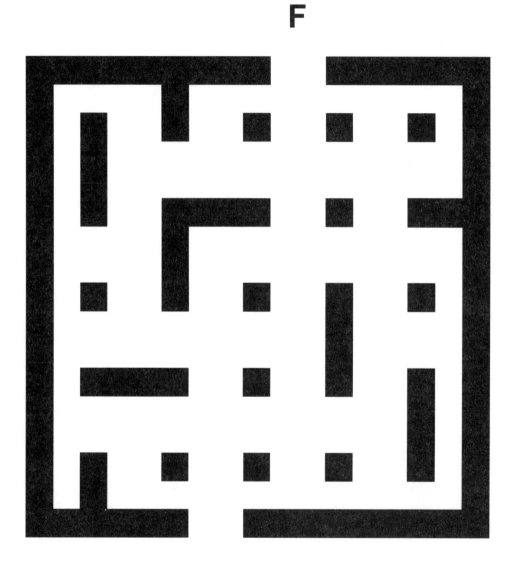

S

MAZE 90

Only one of the 3 pieces (labeled A, B, and C) will allow you to go from start to finish without getting stuck. Which one is it?

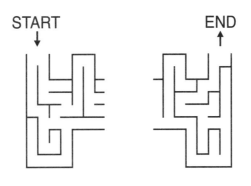

A

B

C

MAZE 91

Don't let the squares confuse you. You can mosey from start to finish in a flash. Take the fastest route.

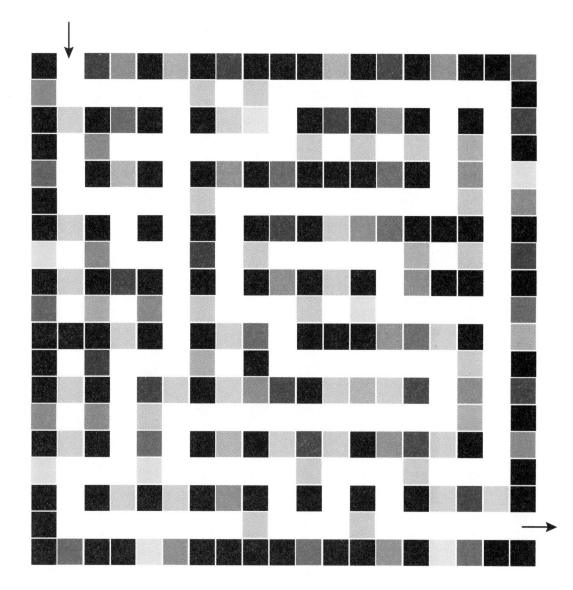

MAZE 92

You're on a runaway train that won't stop moving forward! The path from start to finish must follow the curve of the loops; sharp turns aren't allowed.

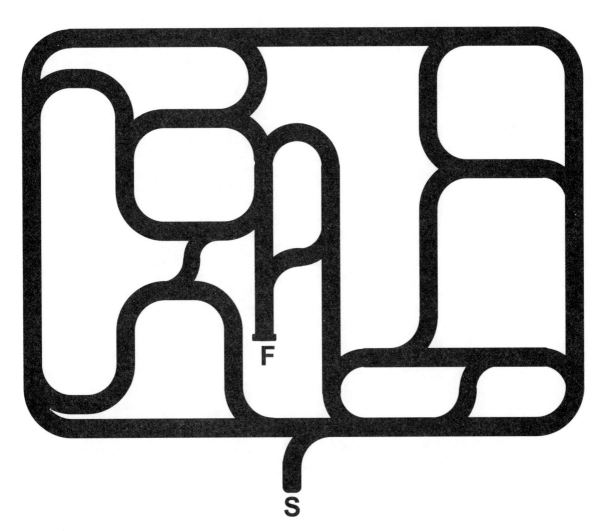

MAZE 93

Don't get too caught up in all the twists and turns as you negotiate your way to the center of this intricate labyrinth.

MAZE 94

You've caught something! Guide your line to the surface and retrieve the fish.

MAZE 95

You've heard this story a million times—a guy gets caught in the belly of a whale. Help him find his way out.

MAZE 96

Guide the elephant from outside the ark to its proper place within.

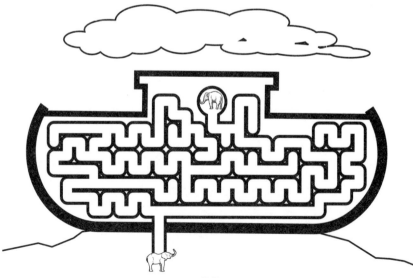

MAZE 97

Guide your way through the tangles of this circuitry maze.

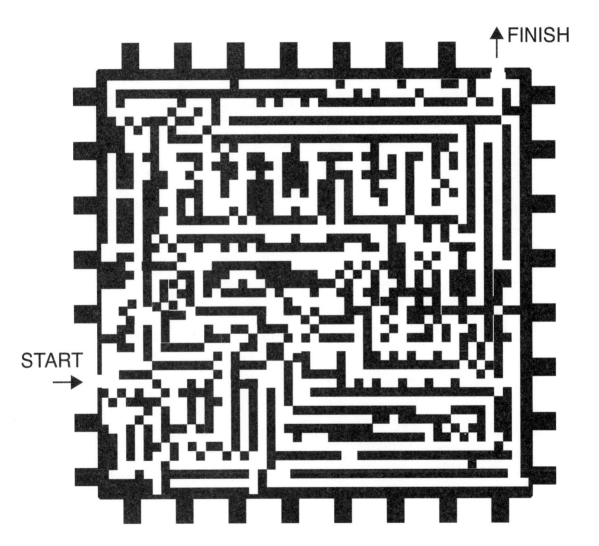

START →

↑ FINISH

MAZE 98

Professor Stanley is trying to find a safe path to the nest of the Klum-Klum bird. Can you help him?

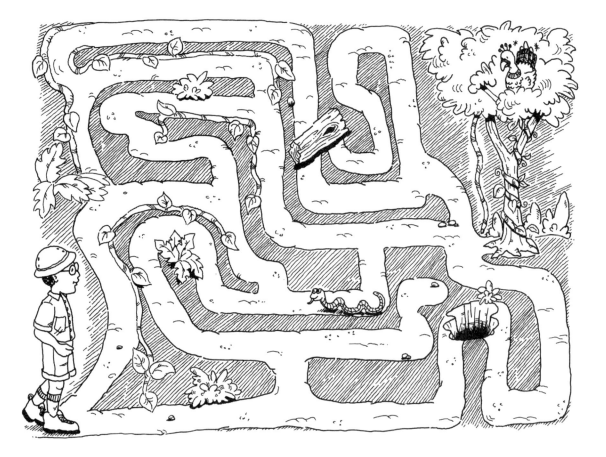

MAZE 99

Navigate the twisting path to find your way through this maze.

end

start

MAZE 100

Help Mary find her way to the food court to meet her friend.

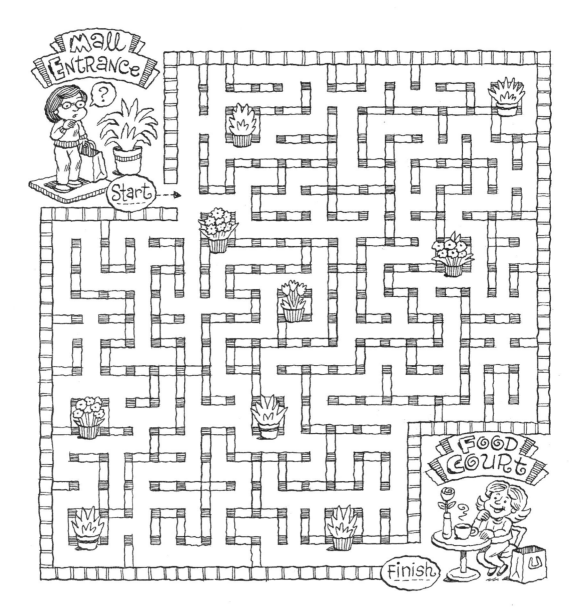

MAZE 101

Follow the ball as it curves its way towards the batter's swing.

MAZE 102

You're on a runaway train that won't stop moving forward! The path from start to finish must follow the curve of the loops; sharp turns aren't allowed.

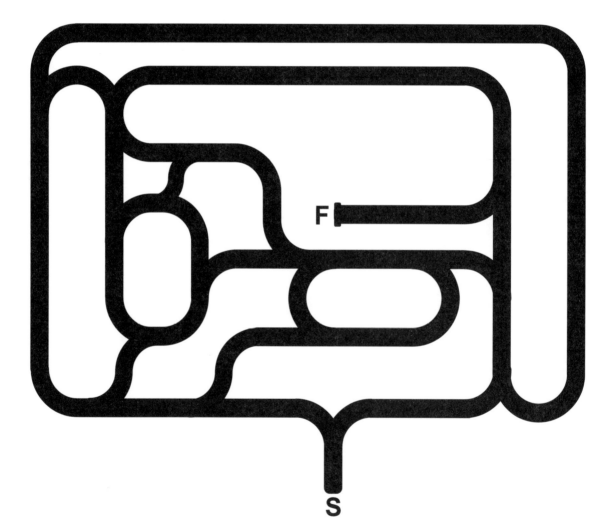

MAZE 103

Find your way through the maze with the fewest number of bounces. Keep going forward until your way is blocked; at that point, you can only turn left or right.

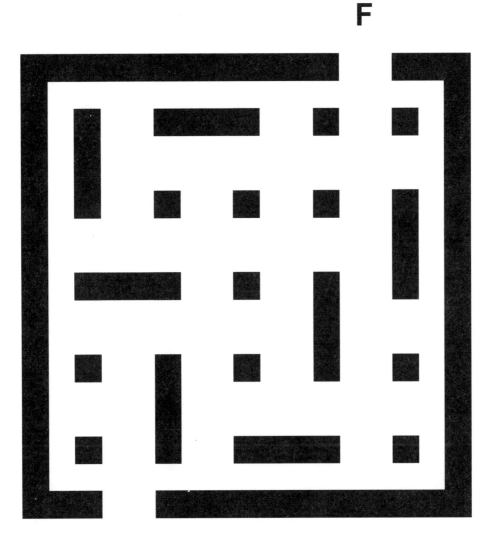

Weave through the windmill's maze. Start and finish with the arrows on the bottom.

MAZE 105

Guide your paintbrush from the bottom to the easel at the top to finish your painting and get out of the maze.

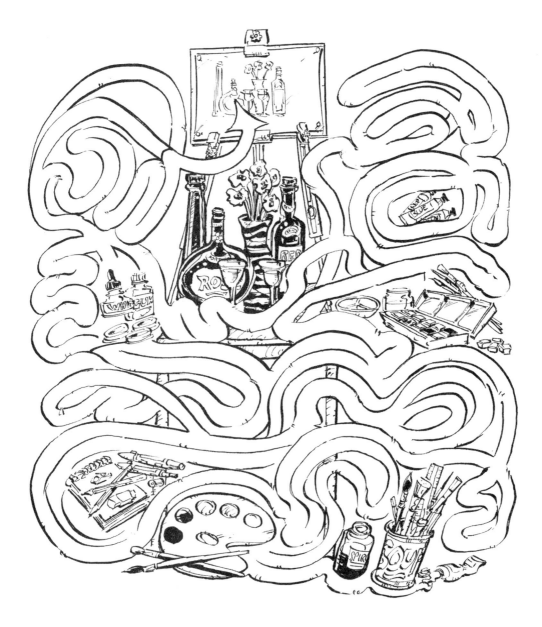

MAZE 106

Navigate this maze from the entrance at left to the exit at right.

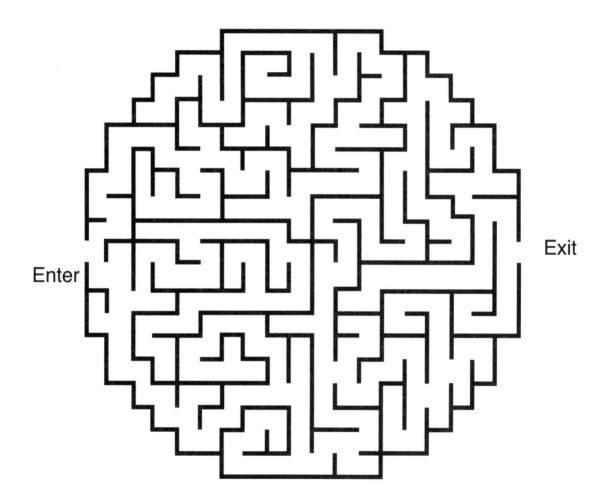

Enter

Exit

Your tractor is jammed and you can only go forward or turn left!

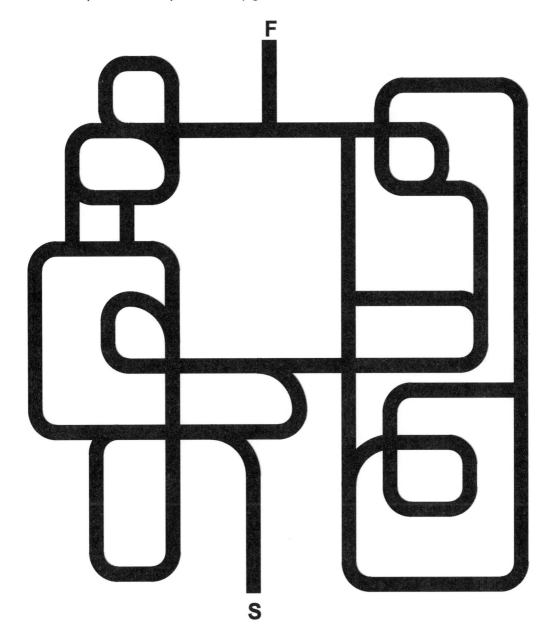

MAZE 108

Only one of the 3 pieces (labeled A, B, and C) will allow you to go from start to finish without getting stuck. Which one is it?

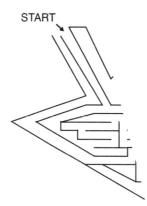

A

B

C

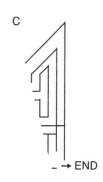

MAZE 109

Cross over and under bridges to reach the end of this maze.

▼start

end ▼

MAZE 110

Watch out for molten lava on your way to the volcano.

START

MAZE 111

Navigate the twisting path to find your way through this maze.

end

start

MAZE 112

Something about this spherical maze reminds us of a basketball. See if you can dribble your way from the entrance on the left side to the exit on the right side.

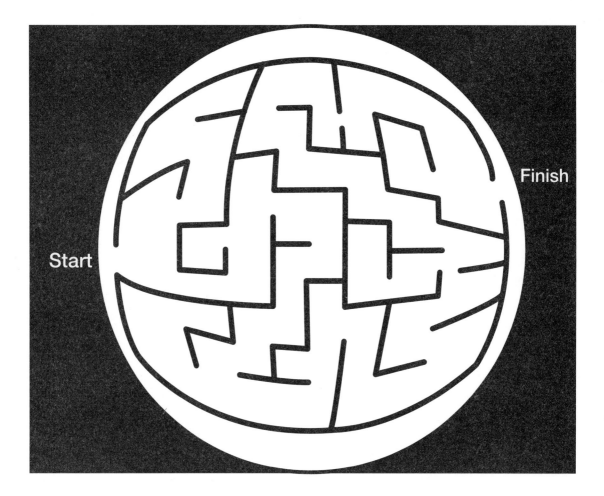

MAZE 113

Stroll through the cottage walk to find the heart. Start at the arrow in the lower left corner.

MAZE 114

Find your way through the maze with the fewest number of bounces. Keep going forward until your way is blocked; at that point, you can only turn left or right.

F

S

MAZE 115

Speed your way through the maze from the top flags to the bottom flag.

MAZE 116

You're on a runaway train that won't stop moving forward! The path from start to finish must follow the curve of the loops; sharp turns aren't allowed.

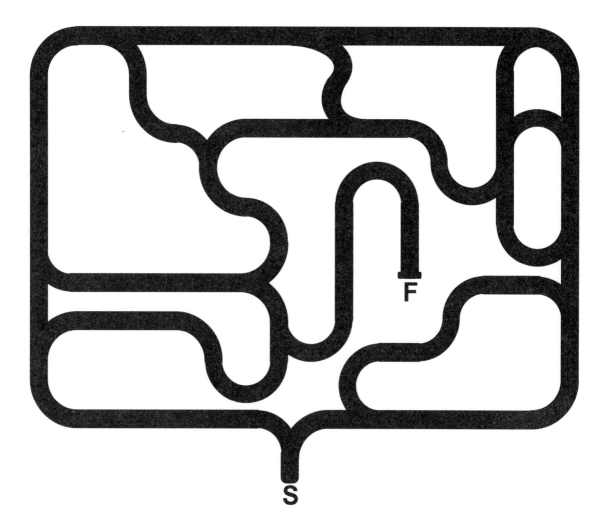

MAZE 117

Follow the electric path from the start to points 1, 2, and 3 in order. Turn on the lightbulb at the end to exit. It is okay to retrace your steps.

MAZE 118

See if you can find your way out of this one!

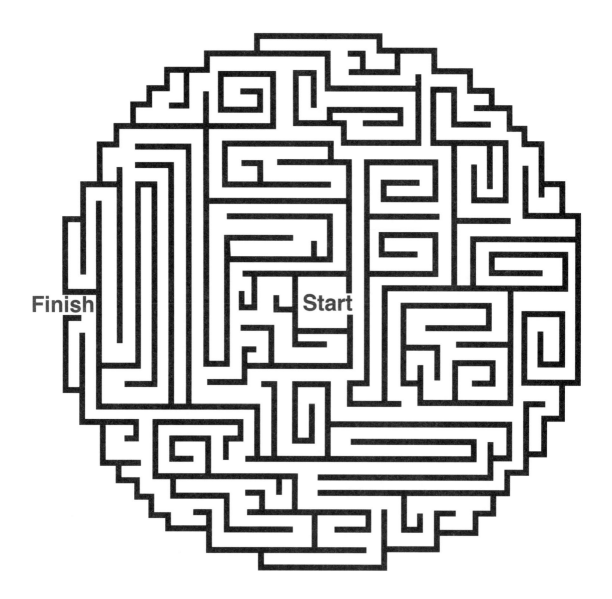

MAZE 119

The taxi meter is ticking. This professional building is a maze of corridors and cubicles. Elevators are available, but there are no stairs. And over-stressed office workers won't give you directions to the exit. Why, oh why, did you ever come in here? Doesn't matter now—time to get moving!

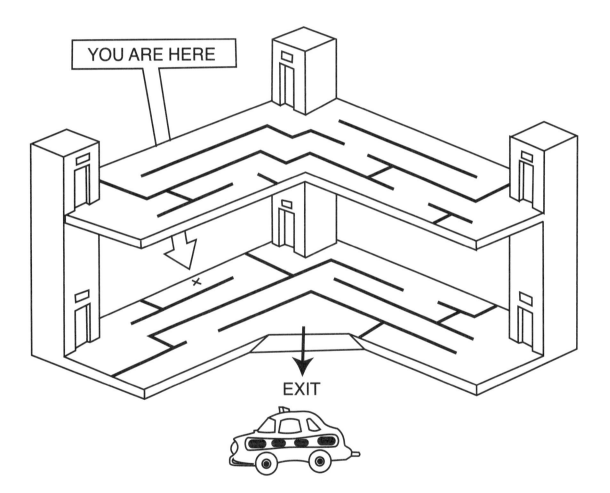

YOU ARE HERE

EXIT

MAZE 120

Follow the ball as it curves its way towards the batter's swing.

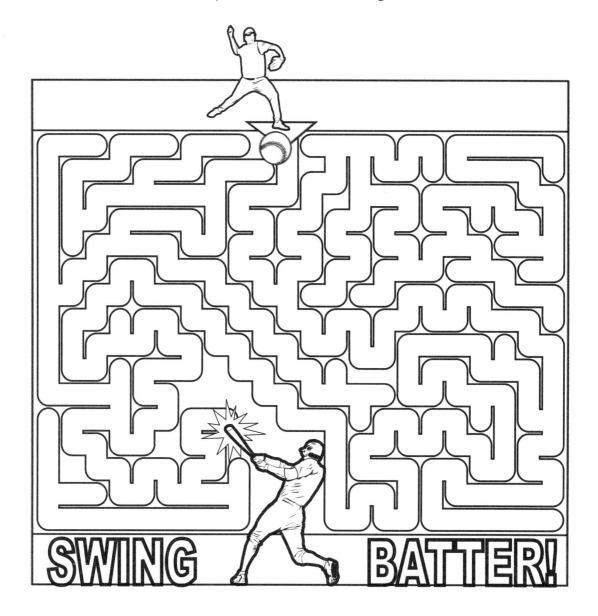

MAZE 121

Find your way out of the kaleidoscope before someone shakes it and you get all pixilated.

START   FINISH

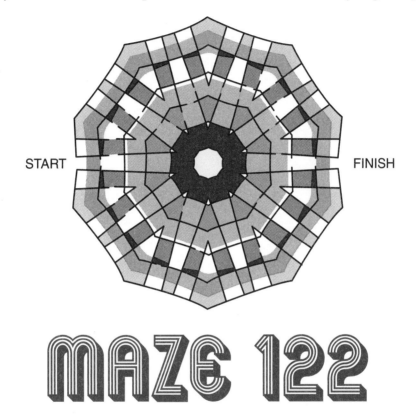

MAZE 122

Can you find the only way to the bars of gold in the center?

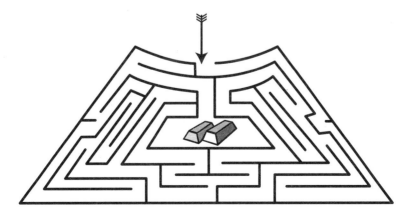

MAZE 123

You're going to have to dig your way out of this maze!

MAZE 124

Watch out for black holes as you help this alien go back to his home planet.

MAZE 125

You'll have to move pretty quickly to get to the helicopter before the lava does!

MAZE 126

This professional building is a maze of corridors and cubicles. Elevators are local or express only; there are no stairs. And over-stressed office workers won't give you directions to the exit. Why, oh why, did you ever come in here? Doesn't matter now because it's time to get moving—the taxi meter is ticking!

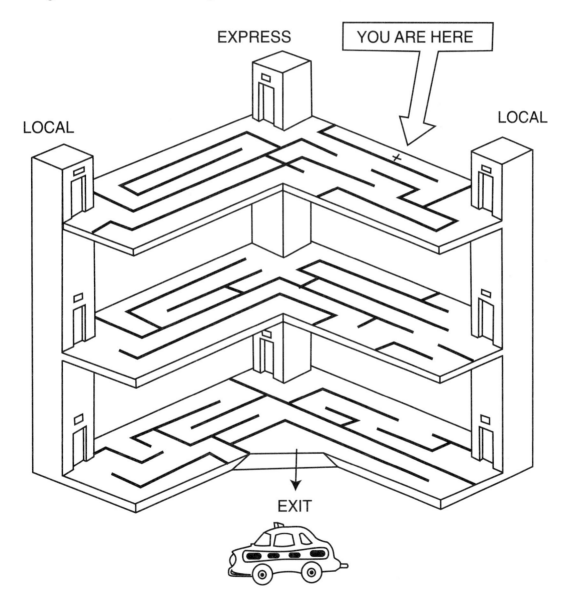

MAZE 127

Guide the net through the swishing waters to capture the fish below!

MAZE 128

Find your way to the inner chamber of this complex cave. You can go under bridges.

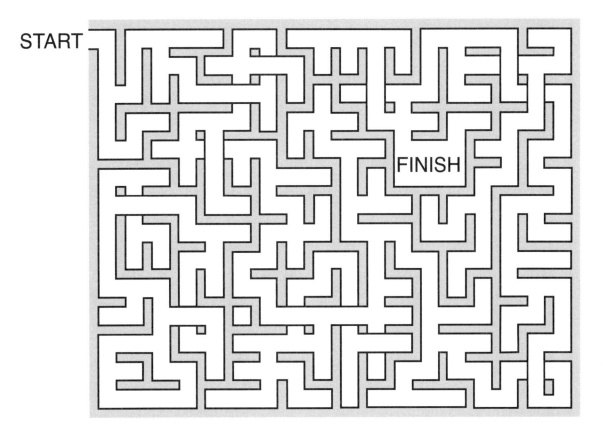

START

FINISH

MAZE 129

There's only one way to get to the treasure at the bottom of this boat—see if you can find it before someone else does! Use the ladders to move from level to level.

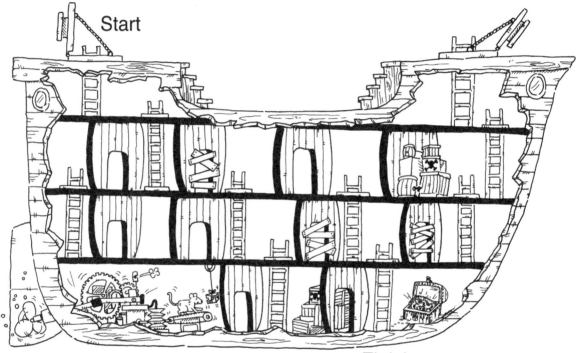

Start

Finish

MAZE 130

Navigate the twisting path to find your way through this maze.

start ▼

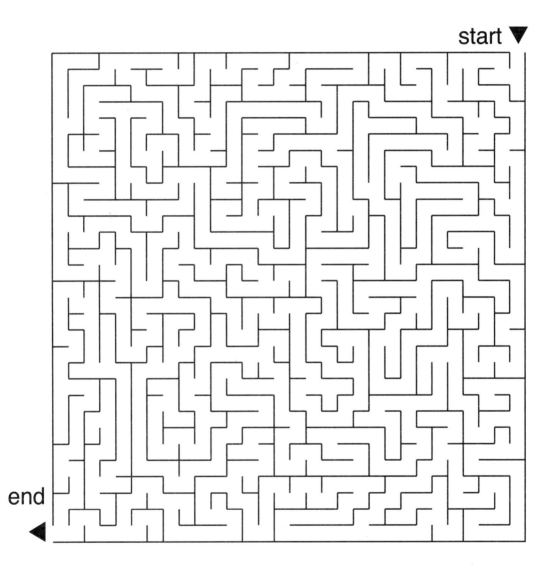

end ◀

MAZE 131

Negotiate your way through this cowboy labyrinth.

MAZE 132

Avoid flying debris as you guide this bird through and then out of the tornado.

MAZE 133

Get the spaceship to the star at the top right corner of the page by moving through alternating shapes. You can move either vertically or horizontally.

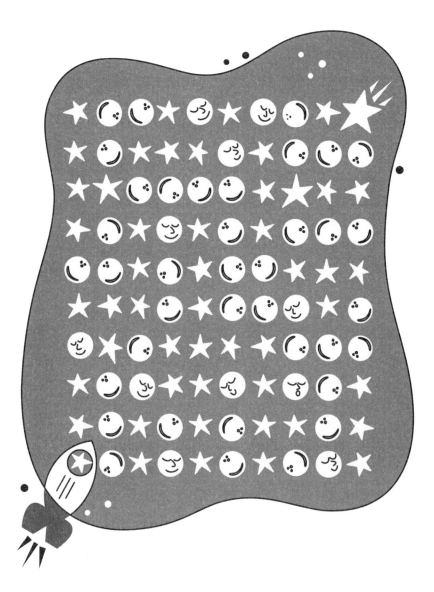

MAZE 134

Only one of the 3 pieces (labeled A, B, and C) will allow you to go from start to finish without getting stuck. Which one is it?

START→

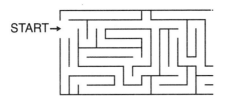

A

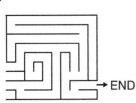
→ END

B

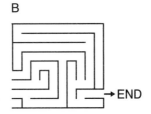
→ END

C

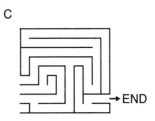
→ END

MAZE 135

START

FINISH

MAZE 136

Your tractor is jammed and you can only go forward or turn left! Can you find your way through the fields?

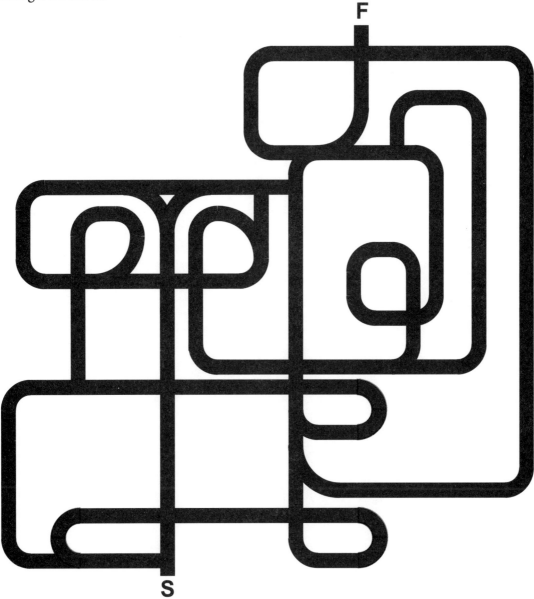

MAZE 137

Navigate the twisting path to find your way through this maze.

start

end

MAZE 138

Picture this maze as a tasty cake. Your goal is the same as for any baked good—get from the outside to the center as quickly as possible, but don't slip on the frosting!

MAZE 139

The taxi meter is ticking. This professional building is a maze of corridors and cubicles. Elevators are available, but there are no stairs. And over-stressed office workers won't give you directions to the exit. Why, oh why, did you ever come in here? Doesn't matter now—time to get moving!

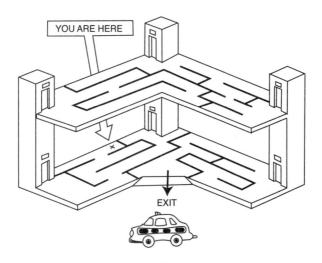

MAZE 140

How fast can Mom get dinner on the table?

MAZE 141

Help the astronaut land on the moon by navigating his spaceship through the solar system.

MAZE 142

Navigate your way from top to bottom.

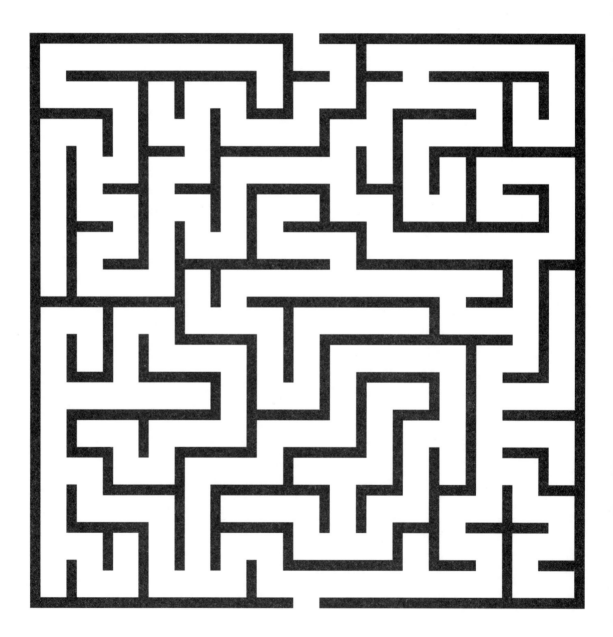

MAZE 143

Guide the elephant through the maze to the peanuts.

MAZE 144

Guide the hang glider to the "X" at the bottom.

MAZE 145

Help the dog reach the bone in the center.

MAZE 146

Find the path from the bird to the worm.

MAZE 147

Follow the archer's path to the center of the maze.

MAZE 148

You'll buzz right through the center of this maze.

MAZE 149

Wind your way to the center of this maze.

MAZE 150

Wind your way over and under to solve this maze.

MAZE 151

Can you find your way through this tangled maze?

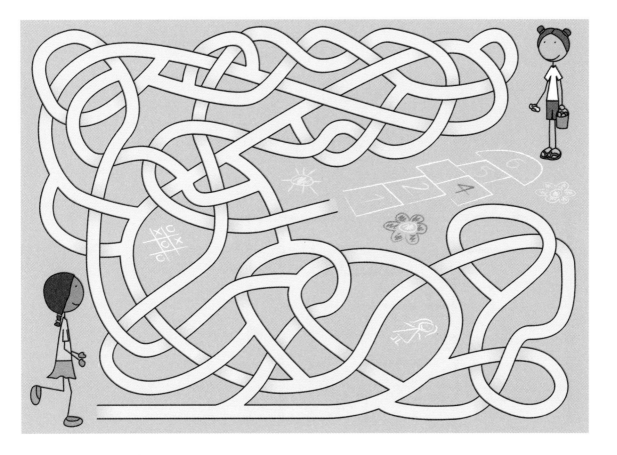

MAZE 152

Hurry the hedgehog through this maze.

MAZE 153

You'll fly right through this maze.

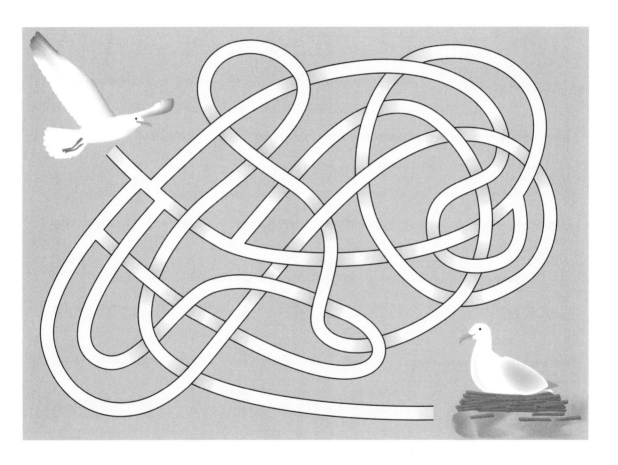

MAZE 154

Guide the fish back to its bowl.

MAZE 155

Make your way to the center of this circle maze.

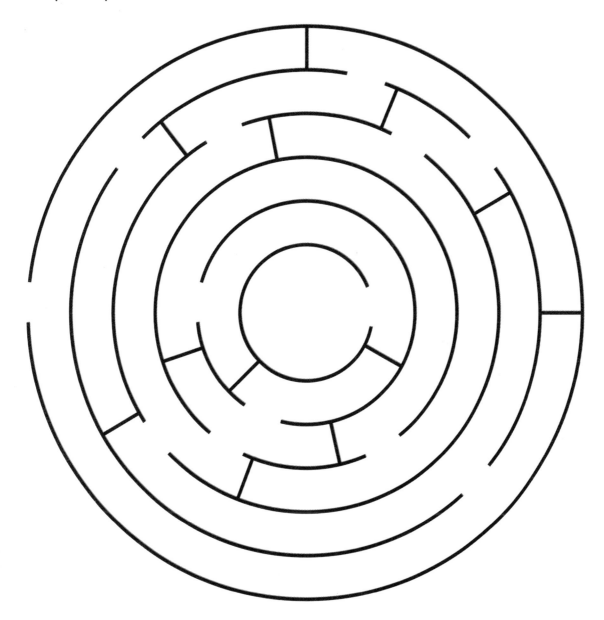

Follow the path to the lost city.

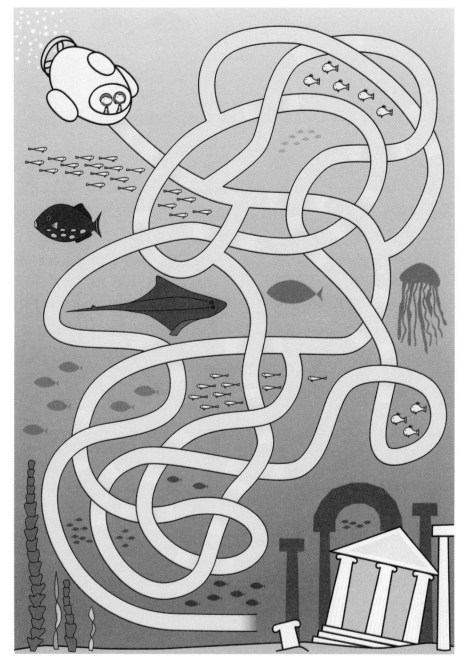

MAZE 157

Guide the ghost out of this maze.

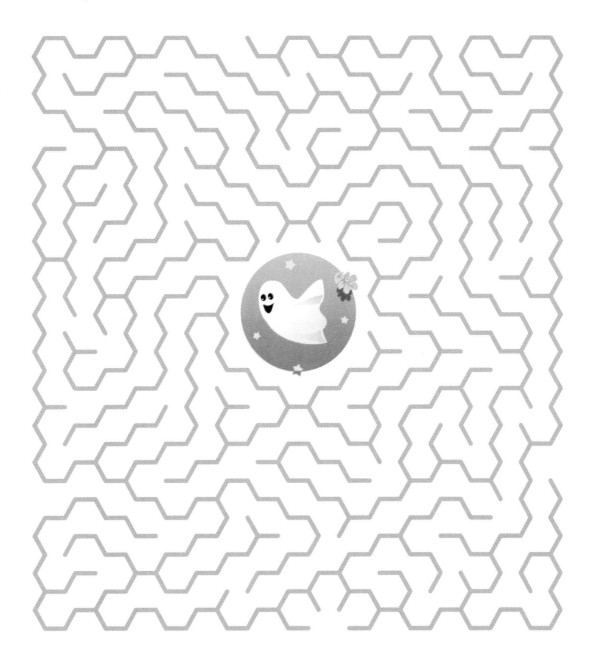

MAZE 158

Guide the girl through the maze to reach the kitten.

MAZE 159

Help the bird reach the birdhouse.

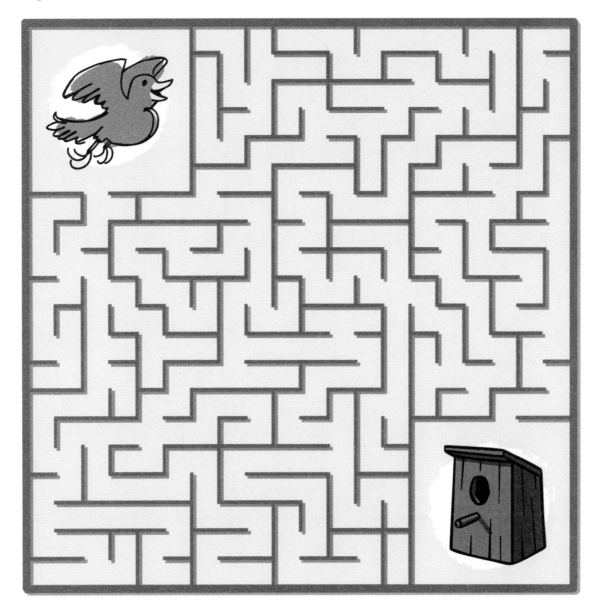

MAZE 160

How quickly can you guide the dog to the bone?

MAZE 161

Help the bear reach the honey on the other side.

MAZE 162

Make your way through this monster maze.

START ➡

GOAL ⬅

MAZE 163

Find your way to the center of this circular maze.

MAZE 164

How fast can you lead the bee to the beehive?

You'll float right through this balloon maze.

MAZE 166

Help the doctor reach his sick patient.

MAZE 1

C

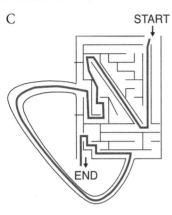

MAZE 4

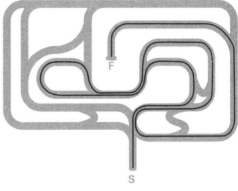

MAZE 2

MAZE 5

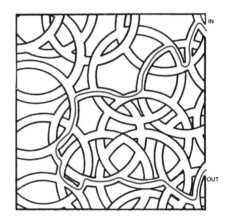

MAZE 3

MAZE 6

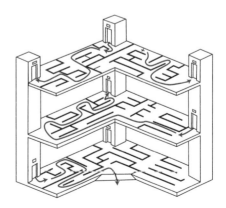

ANSWERS

MAZE 7

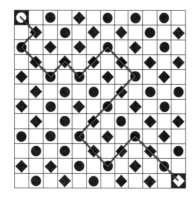

MAZE 10

MAZE 8

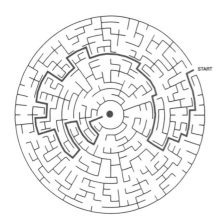

MAZE 11

MAZE 9

MAZE 12

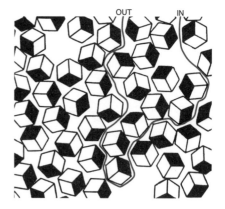

MAZE 13

MAZE 16

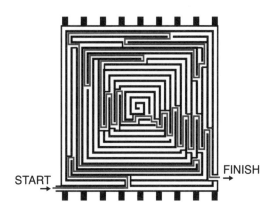

START ➡

FINISH ➡

MAZE 14

MAZE 17

MAZE 15

MAZE 18

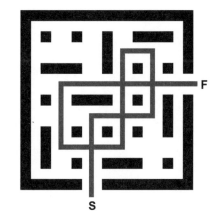

F

S

ANSWERS

MAZE 19

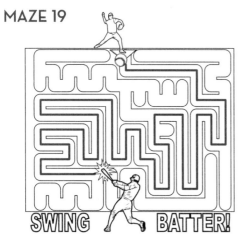

MAZE 22

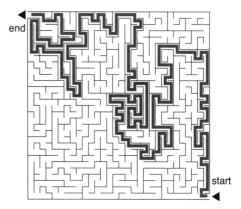

MAZE 20

B

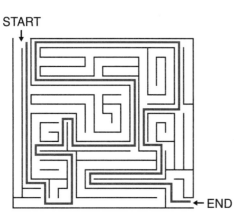

MAZE 23

MAZE 21

MAZE 24

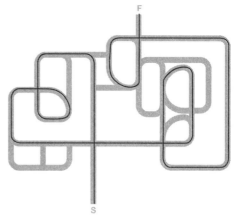

MAZE 25

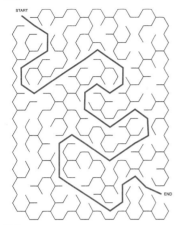

MAZE 26

MAZE 27

MAZE 28

MAZE 29

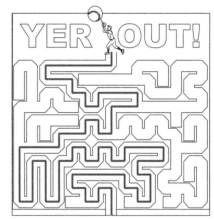

MAZE 30

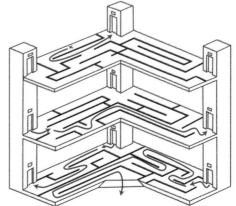

ANSWERS

MAZE 31

MAZE 34

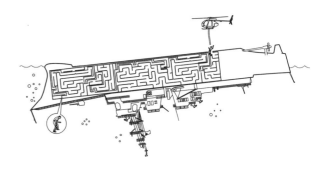

MAZE 32

MAZE 35

MAZE 33

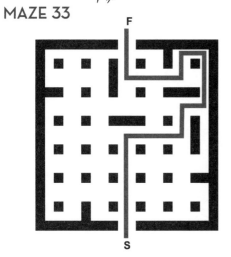

MAZE 36

MAZE 37

MAZE 38

MAZE 39

MAZE 40

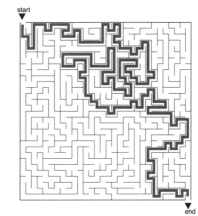

MAZE 41

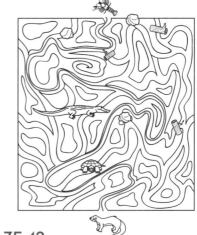

MAZE 42

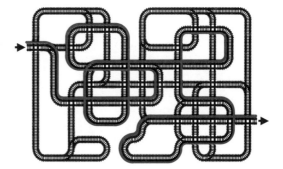

ANSWERS

MAZE 43

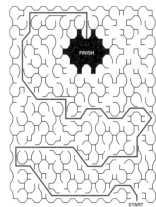

MAZE 46

MAZE 44

MAZE 47

MAZE 45

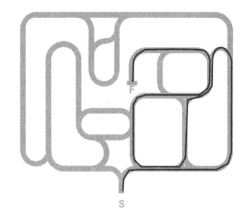

MAZE 48

MAZE 49
A

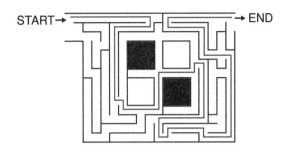

MAZE 50

MAZE 51

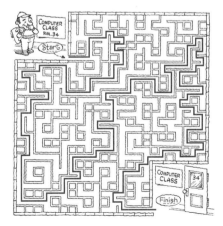

MAZE 52

MAZE 53

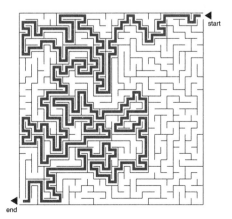

MAZE 54

ANSWERS

MAZE 55

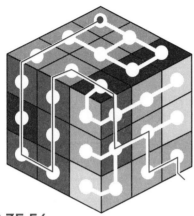

MAZE 56

MAZE 57

MAZE 58

MAZE 59

MAZE 60

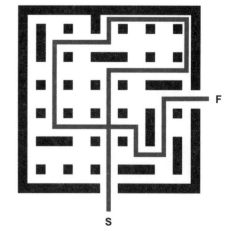

MAZE 61

MAZE 64

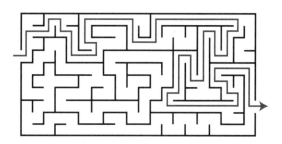

MAZE 62

MAZE 65

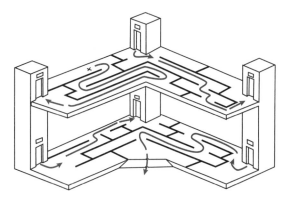

MAZE 63

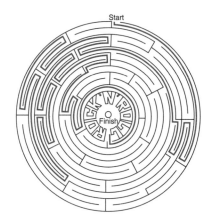

MAZE 66

ANSWERS

MAZE 67

MAZE 68

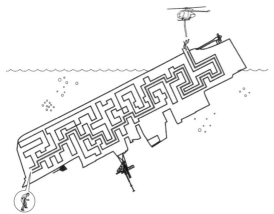

MAZE 69

MAZE 70

MAZE 71

MAZE 72

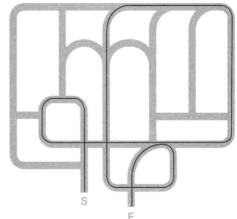

MAZE 73

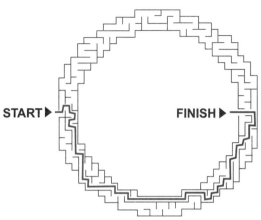

MAZE 76

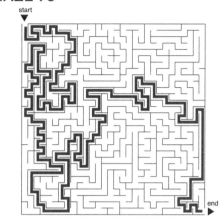

MAZE 74

MAZE 77

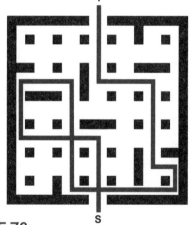

MAZE 75

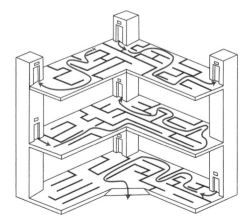

MAZE 78

ANSWERS

MAZE 79

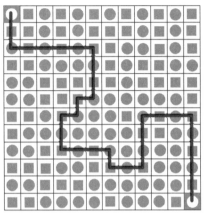

MAZE 82

MAZE 80

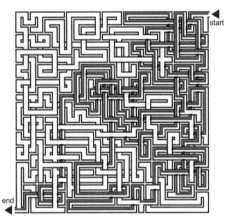

MAZE 83

MAZE 81

MAZE 84

MAZE 85

MAZE 88

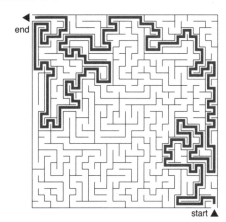

MAZE 86

MAZE 89

MAZE 87

MAZE 90

C

ANSWERS

MAZE 91

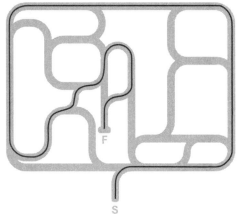

MAZE 92

MAZE 93

MAZE 94

MAZE 95

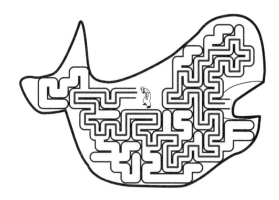

MAZE 96

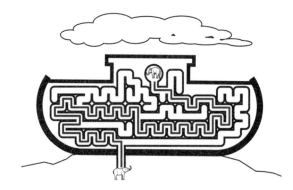

MAZE 97

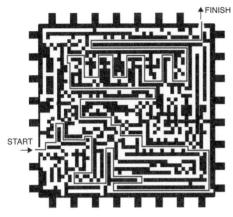

START →
↑FINISH

MAZE 100

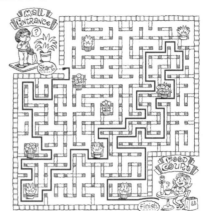

MAZE 98

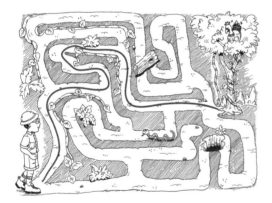

MAZE 101

MAZE 99

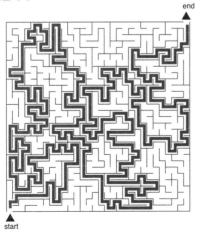

end ▲
▲ start

MAZE 102

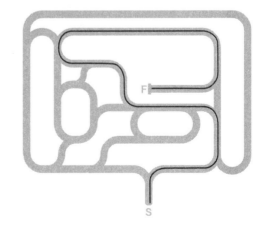

ANSWERS

MAZE 103

MAZE 104

MAZE 105

MAZE 106

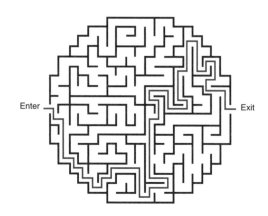

MAZE 107

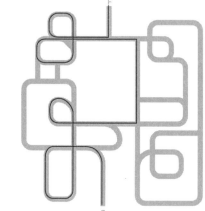

MAZE 108

A

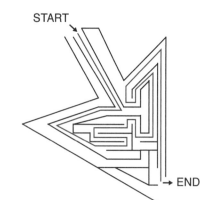

MAZE 109

MAZE 112

MAZE 110

MAZE 113

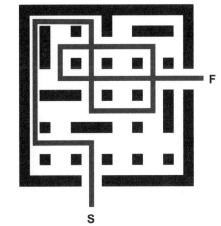

MAZE 111

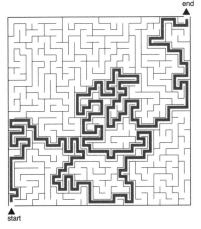

MAZE 114

ANSWERS

MAZE 115

MAZE 118

MAZE 116

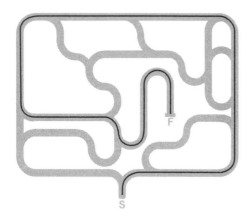

MAZE 119

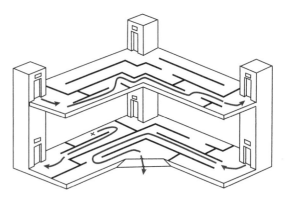

MAZE 117

MAZE 120

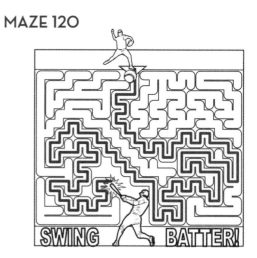

MAZE 121

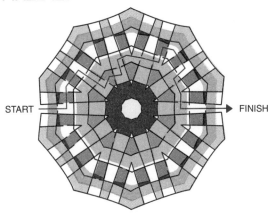

MAZE 124

MAZE 122

MAZE 125

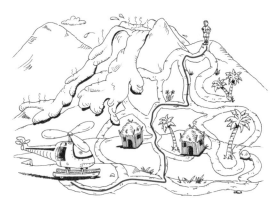

MAZE 123

MAZE 126

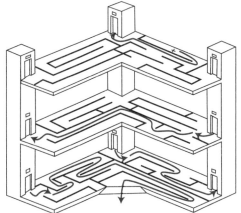

ANSWERS

MAZE 127

MAZE 128

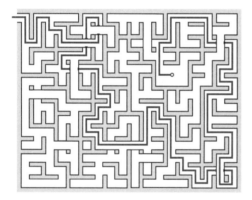

MAZE 129

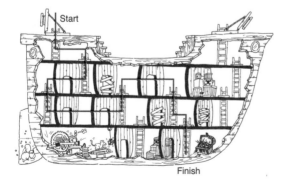

MAZE 130

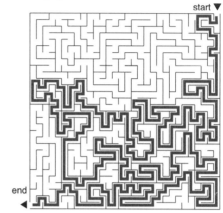

MAZE 131

MAZE 132

MAZE 133

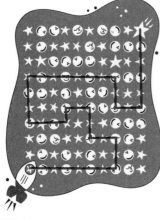

MAZE 136

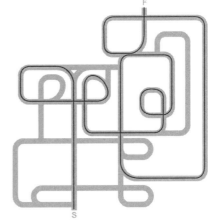

MAZE 134

B

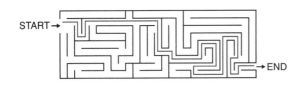

MAZE 137

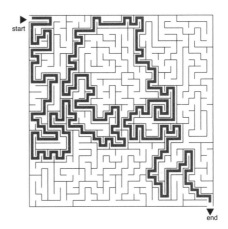

MAZE 135

MAZE 138

ANSWERS

MAZE 139

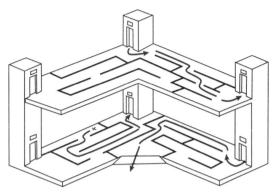

MAZE 142

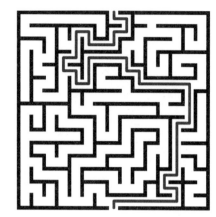

MAZE 140

MAZE 143

MAZE 141

MAZE 144

MAZE 145

MAZE 148

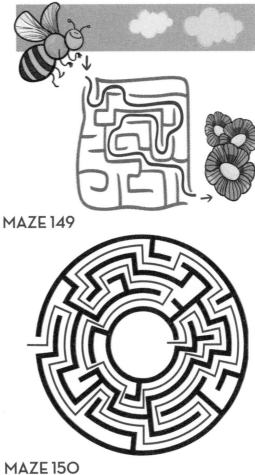

MAZE 146

MAZE 149

MAZE 147

MAZE 150

ANSWERS

MAZE 151

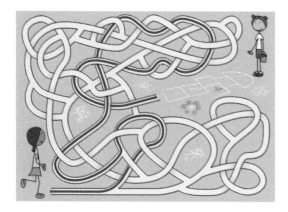

MAZE 154

MAZE 152

MAZE 155

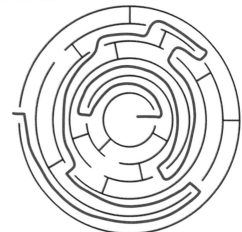

MAZE 153

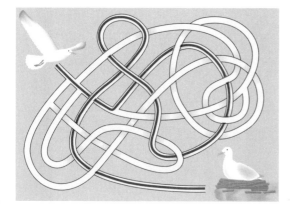

MAZE 156

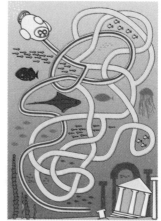

MAZE 157

MAZE 160

MAZE 158

MAZE 161

MAZE 159

MAZE 162

ANSWERS

MAZE 163

MAZE 165

MAZE 164

MAZE 166